WHAT IS A PLANET?

JEFF MAPUA

Britannica
Educational Publishing

IN ASSOCIATION WITH

ROSEN
EDUCATIONAL SERVICES

Published in 2015 by Britannica Educational Publishing (a trademark of Encyclopædia Britannica, Inc.) in association with The Rosen Publishing Group, Inc.
29 East 21st Street, New York, NY 10010

Distributed exclusively by Rosen Publishing.

To see additional Britannica Educational Publishing titles, go to rosenpublishing.com.

First Edition

Britannica Educational Publishing
J.E. Luebering: Director, Core Reference Group
Mary Rose McCudden: Editor, Britannica Student Encylopedia

Rosen Publishing
Hope Lourie Killcoyne: Executive Editor
John Kemmerer: Editor
Nelson Sá: Art Director
Michael Moy: Designer
Cindy Reiman: Photography Manager
Karen Huang: Photo Researcher

Cataloging-in-Publication Data

Mapua, Jeff, author.
What is a planet?/Jeff Mapua. — First edition.
     pages cm. — (Let's find out! Space)
Includes bibliographical references and index.
ISBN 978-1-62275-456-4 (library bound) — ISBN 978-1-62275-458-8 (pbk.) — ISBN 978-1-62275-459-5 (6-pack)
1. Planets—Juvenile literature. I. Title.
QB602.M335 2015
523.2 — dc23
                                                                    2013051264

CONTENTS

WHAT IS A PLANET?

The word "planet" comes from the Greek word *planetes*, which means "wanderer." Planets are large natural objects that orbit, or travel around, stars. Eight planets orbit the star called the Sun. In order from the closest to

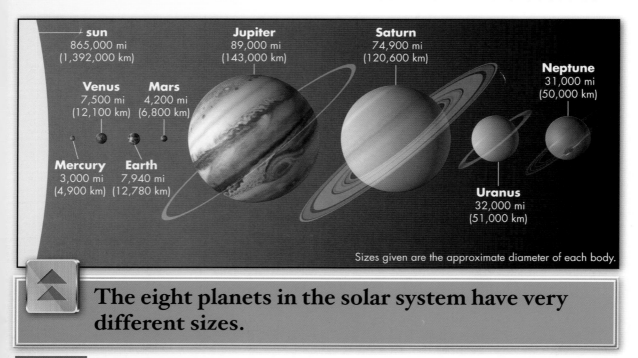

sun
865,000 mi
(1,392,000 km)

Jupiter
89,000 mi
(143,000 km)

Saturn
74,900 mi
(120,600 km)

Neptune
31,000 mi
(50,000 km)

Venus
7,500 mi
(12,100 km)

Mars
4,200 mi
(6,800 km)

Mercury
3,000 mi
(4,900 km)

Earth
7,940 mi
(12,780 km)

Uranus
32,000 mi
(51,000 km)

Sizes given are the approximate diameter of each body.

The eight planets in the solar system have very different sizes.

the Sun, these planets are Mercury, Venus, Earth, Mars, Jupiter, Saturn, Uranus, and Neptune. The solar system is the collection of the Sun and the objects that orbit around it, including the eight planets.

Planets differ from other objects such as comets, asteroids, and meteors. In general, planets are the largest objects in the solar system after the Sun. Most of them orbit the Sun in a path shaped nearly like a circle. Many also have a layer of gas surrounding them. Most of the planets have at least one moon. Jupiter has more than 60 moons.

COMPARE AND CONTRAST

There are different objects orbiting the Sun. Compare and contrast planets, comets, and meteors.

Io, a moon of Jupiter, has an active volcano, like ones on Earth.

TYPES OF PLANETS

There are two main types of planets in the solar system. The four planets nearest the Sun—Mercury, Venus, Earth, and Mars—are called inner planets. They are also called the Earth-like planets. The inner planets are rocky and about the size of Earth or somewhat

Earth is the only planet in the solar system known to have liquid water on its surface.

smaller. They each have solid surfaces. None of these planets has rings, and only Earth and Mars have moons.

Jupiter, Saturn, Uranus, and Neptune are called gas giants. They are made up mostly of gases and have no solid surfaces. They are all much larger than Earth. Each of the four has a large atmosphere, or surrounding layer of gases. Also, the gas giants each have many moons and a system of rings. Saturn's rings are the largest and best known.

Saturn's unique rings are mostly made of ice and dust.

An **atmosphere** is a layer of gases surrounding a planet.

FORMATION OF PLANETS

Most scientists believe our solar system began to develop about 4.6 billion years ago. It probably started as a loose

cloud of gas and dust. Scientists think that a force called gravity pulled parts of the cloud together into clumps. The clumps squeezed so tightly together that they became hot. The cloud, called the solar nebula, changed shape into a spinning disk and grew even hotter.

The largest clump eventually became the Sun. The planets

The Eagle Nebula is a giant cloud of cold gas and dust. Our solar system was once a nebula like this one.

developed from the remaining material of the cloud. The disk then began to cool down. Gases in the disk combined into solid objects. The solid objects combined into bigger objects and attracted more material in a process called accretion. Over time, much of the material clumped together into larger bodies called planetesimals. They eventually formed even larger bodies, which, in turn, developed into planets.

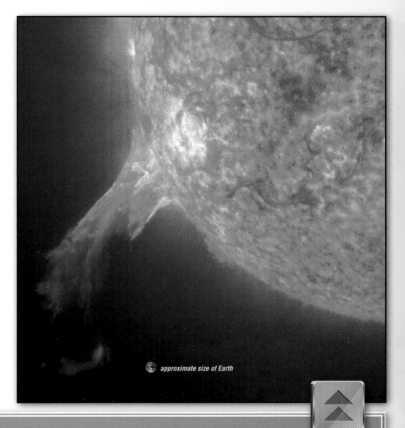

approximate size of Earth

The Sun is the largest object in our solar system. It can fit 1,300,000 Earths inside of it.

Scientists developed theories about the formation of the planets based on observations of the solar system. The interior of the solar nebula—a giant cloud of gas and dust—had hotter temperatures near the Sun than farther away from the center. Metals and rocks formed from the original cloud of gas and dust. These metal and rock objects formed the inner, rocky planets.

Farther away from the hot center near the Sun, temperatures were cold enough for ice to form. The ice in the outer planets is made of substances such as

Kepler's Nova is a nebula formed from the explosion of a dying star.

water, carbon dioxide, and ammonia. The outer planets grew bigger because of the ice and attracted light elements like hydrogen and helium. These are the most common elements in the universe, so the outer planets were able to grow to large sizes.

More than 1,000 Earths could fit inside Jupiter. The black dot is its moon Europa, which is close to the size of Earth's moon.

Think About It

The disk of gas spinning around the still-developing Sun formed the planets. Why do the planets in our solar system orbit in the same direction?

EVOLUTION OF PLANETS

The early solar system began when a giant cloud of gas and dust collapsed and began spinning and getting hotter. The planets began as planetesimals. Then they grew into **protoplanets**. The early solar system was very violent. Planetesimals and other forming planets collided with each other. Scientists believe the moon was made when a large piece of Earth broke off after hitting another planetesimal.

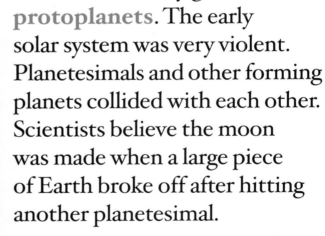

This computer model shows what the solar system looked like early in its formation.

Protoplanets were moon-sized or larger clumps of material that became the planets we see today.

Protoplanets combined with other pieces of matter floating in space and grew bigger. The interiors grew hot and melted. Heavier rocks sank to the center of planets, and lighter rocks were pushed upward. This is called differentiation. These lighter rocks formed the crusts of planets, like the outer part of Earth. Lighter elements like hydrogen, helium, and oxygen became atmospheres or oceans.

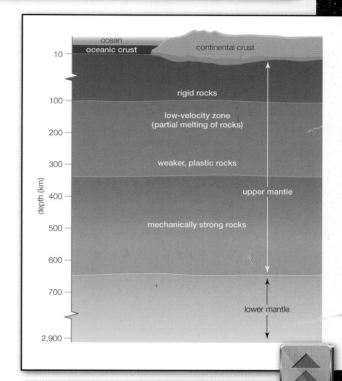

Earth is made up of layers of rocks, with the heaviest rocks near the core.

ORBITS OF PLANETS

The solar system's planets move through space in two basic ways at the same time. They orbit the Sun, and they rotate on their axes (plural of "axis"). So they each spin like a top while also circling the Sun. The path each planet travels around the Sun is called an orbit. The eight planets orbit the Sun in the same direction as the Sun's rotation. The planets' orbits trace a large disk around the Sun's equator. Mercury's orbit is the most tilted.

The planets' orbits are not perfect circles. They are slightly

The path a planet takes around the Sun is called an orbit.

oval. The orbits form a type of closed curve called an ellipse. Mercury has the most eccentric, or least circular, orbit of the planets. Venus and Neptune have the most circular orbits. Planets move faster when their orbits bring them closer to the Sun and more slowly when they are farther away.

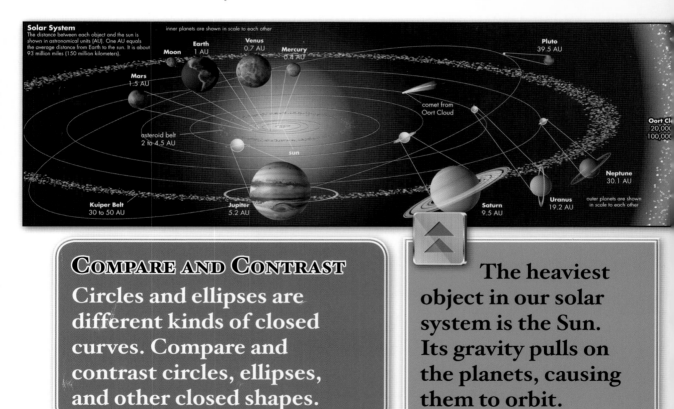

Solar System
The distance between each object and the sun is shown in astronomical units (AU). One AU equals the average distance from Earth to the sun. It is about 93 million miles (150 million kilometers).

inner planets are shown in scale to each other

Moon
Earth
1 AU
Venus
0.7 AU
Mercury
0.4 AU
Pluto
39.5 AU
Mars
1.5 AU
comet from
Oort Cloud
Oort Cl
20,000
100,000
asteroid belt
2 to 4.5 AU
sun
Neptune
30.1 AU
Kuiper Belt
30 to 50 AU
Jupiter
5.2 AU
Saturn
9.5 AU
Uranus
19.2 AU
outer planets are shown
in scale to each other

COMPARE AND CONTRAST
Circles and ellipses are different kinds of closed curves. Compare and contrast circles, ellipses, and other closed shapes.

The heaviest object in our solar system is the Sun. Its gravity pulls on the planets, causing them to orbit.

ROTATIONS OF PLANETS

The planets of our solar system orbit the Sun while also rotating on their axes. Each planet rotates, or spins about its center. Most of the planets rotate in the same direction in which they orbit the Sun. Only Venus and Uranus rotate in the opposite direction, which is called retrograde rotation. As planets spin, their different sides rotate toward the Sun (daytime) and then away from the Sun (nighttime).

In addition to having different orbits, planets also rotate in different ways.

Mercury and Venus are different because they spin on their axes slowly. By the time they each complete one rotation, they have traveled very far in their orbit around the Sun. In fact, a day (the time it takes to spin around once on the axis) on Venus is longer than a year (the time it takes to orbit once around the Sun) on Venus. One day on Mercury lasts roughly two-thirds of a year, while there is only about one day in the year on Venus.

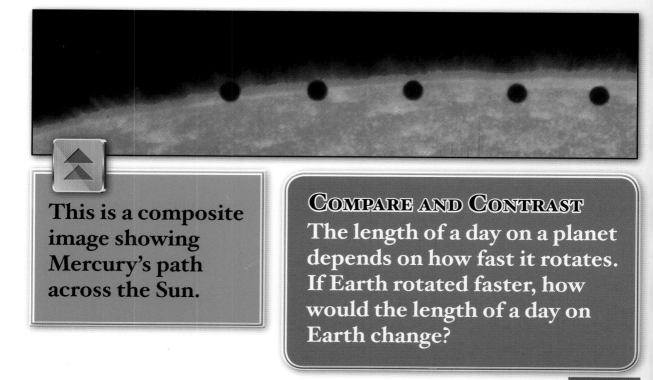

This is a composite image showing Mercury's path across the Sun.

COMPARE AND CONTRAST
The length of a day on a planet depends on how fast it rotates. If Earth rotated faster, how would the length of a day on Earth change?

DAYS, YEARS, AND SEASONS

As a planet spins, it turns different portions of its surface toward and then away from the Sun. In one day, a person on the planet would seem to see the Sun rise, travel overhead, set, and then rise again. A day is equal to the time it takes the planet to complete one rotation. The length of a day is different on every planet. Earth completes one rotation in about 24 hours.

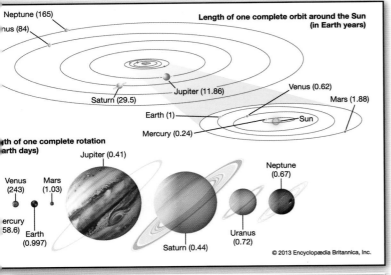

Neptune (165)
nus (84)

Length of one complete orbit around the Sun (in Earth years)

Saturn (29.5)
Jupiter (11.86)
Venus (0.62)
Mars (1.88)
Earth (1)
Mercury (0.24)
Sun

th of one complete rotation
arth days)
Jupiter (0.41)
Neptune (0.67)
Venus (243)
Mars (1.03)
ercury (58.6)
Earth (0.997)
Uranus (0.72)
Saturn (0.44)

© 2013 Encyclopædia Britannica, Inc.

Planets rotate and orbit the Sun at different speeds.

The time it takes a planet to complete one orbit around the Sun is equal to a year on that planet. For example, Earth completes one orbit every 365 days, so that is how long a year on Earth lasts. Seasons are caused mainly by the tilt of a planet toward the Sun. Mercury, Venus, and Jupiter are barely tilted, so they experience little or no seasonal differences in weather.

COMPARE AND CONTRAST

A year is equal to one complete orbit of a planet around the Sun. Compare and contrast the years of the eight planets in the solar system.

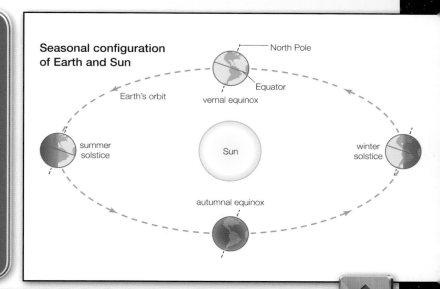

Seasonal configuration of Earth and Sun

North Pole

Equator

Earth's orbit

vernal equinox

summer solstice

Sun

winter solstice

autumnal equinox

This diagram shows how Earth's tilt toward or away from the Sun determines the seasons.

THE INNER PLANETS

Mercury is the smallest planet, and it is the closest planet to the Sun. It travels around the Sun at a faster speed than any other planet. Mercury is very heavy for its size. Venus is Earth's nearest neighbor. Thick clouds always cover the planet. The gases and clouds trap heat. Venus is the hottest planet in the solar system. Venus is about the same size and weight as Earth.

In this color-coded image of Venus, the purple and blue colors show low elevations, while red and white show the highest elevations.

Earth is the only planet in the solar system that can support life because it has water on its surface and oxygen gas in its air. Earth also has the perfect **range** of temperatures for life. Mars is Earth's outer neighbor. Water exists on Mars as ice caps and patches of ice beneath its surface. Scientists are still trying to find out if very tiny, simple life-forms may have ever existed on Mars.

The *Mars Express* spacecraft discovered a patch of ice on Mars's surface.

A range is an area defined by an upper and lower limit.

THE OUTER PLANETS

Jupiter is called a gas giant. It consists almost entirely of gases, mainly hydrogen and helium. In terms of volume, it could contain more than 1,300 Earths. The planet has no solid surface. Jupiter's clouds appear in colored spots and bright and dark stripes. One of the spots is a huge storm called the Great Red Spot. The storm is more than twice as wide as Earth.

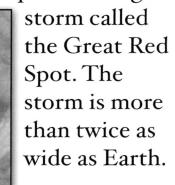

 Jupiter's Great Red Spot was first recorded in 1831.

It is believed to have formed more than 300 years ago and may be permanent.

Saturn is the second-largest planet in the solar system, after Jupiter. However, Saturn is very light for its size. It would float if placed in water. Saturn's center is probably a hot, rocky core. It is known for its beautiful rings. The rings extend thousands of miles out from the planet. They are made up mostly of pieces of rock, ice, and dust.

Italian physicist and mathematician Galileo discovered Saturn's rings in 1610.

Uranus was the first planet to be discovered after the invention of the telescope. Narrow rings surround Uranus. The rings may be made of ice particles coated with some silicates or carbon-based material that give them a dark and reddish hue. Neptune is a stormy world. The planet has the highest winds ever discovered in the solar system. The winds are almost supersonic, meaning they are almost faster than the speed of sound. The planet has no solid surface. Scientists think that Neptune has hot, thick liquids deep inside it.

Scientists used to call Pluto the ninth planet. Pluto is a planetlike

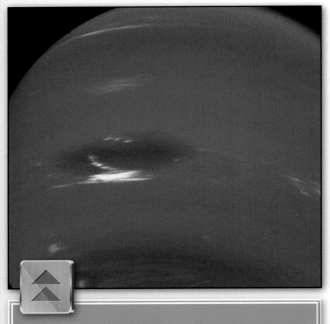

Photos of the storms on Neptune were taken by *Voyager 2* in 1989.

object that is usually situated beyond Neptune. Pluto's orbit is different from those of the eight planets. It overlaps the orbit of Neptune, so Pluto occasionally moves in front of its neighboring planet. Pluto is much smaller than the eight planets. In 2006, a group of scientists decided to make a new category for Pluto and similar objects in the solar system. They called the objects dwarf planets.

Pluto is classified as a plutoid, a spherical object that orbits the Sun but is farther from it than Neptune.

Think About It

Saturn, Uranus, and Neptune have rings. What would a person see in the sky if Earth had rings?

Other Planets

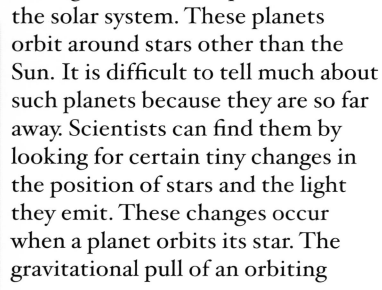

In the 1990s, scientists began to discover planets outside the solar system. These planets orbit around stars other than the Sun. It is difficult to tell much about such planets because they are so far away. Scientists can find them by looking for certain tiny changes in the position of stars and the light they emit. These changes occur when a planet orbits its star. The gravitational pull of an orbiting

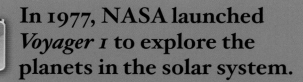

In 1977, NASA launched *Voyager 1* to explore the planets in the solar system.

planet will actually cause a star to move in its own very small orbit. And when a planet crosses in front of its star, it dims the observable light that the star emits.

In solar systems beyond our own, one or more planets orbit a star—just as the eight planets in our solar system orbit the Sun. These planets are called **extrasolar** planets. Finding other planetary systems is not easy, however, because extrasolar planets appear much dimmer than the stars they orbit. As space telescopes become more sensitive, they are likely to discover more extrasolar planets.

Some planets, like the one in this illustration, orbit two stars.

Extrasolar means outside of our solar system.

A Sky Full of Planets

All across the universe, large clouds of dust clumped together and formed solar systems. Planets formed from these clumps. The planets were of many different types, such as small and rocky or large and made of gas. Today, planets rotate at different speeds and can orbit stars for different lengths of time. The weather on the

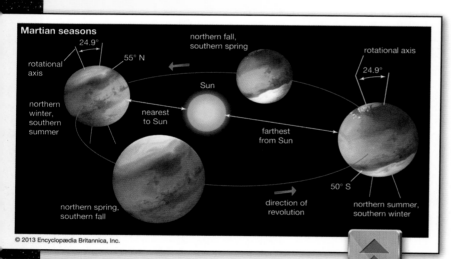

Martian seasons

rotational axis

24.9°

55° N

northern fall, southern spring

rotational axis

24.9°

Sun

northern winter, southern summer

nearest to Sun

farthest from Sun

50° S

northern spring, southern fall

direction of revolution

northern summer, southern winter

© 2013 Encyclopædia Britannica, Inc.

Mars has four seasons based on the way it tilts toward the Sun.

COMPARE AND CONTRAST

Our four seasons depend upon how Earth is tilted toward and away from the Sun. Compare and contrast the weather as Earth tilts toward the Sun, then tilts away from the Sun.

planets depends on how much or how little they tilt toward their nearest star.

Our solar system is only a small part of a huge system of stars and other objects called the Milky Way galaxy. The Milky Way galaxy is just one of billions of other galaxies that make up the universe. There are billions of stars in the universe, and there are even more planets orbiting them. Earth is just one of billions and billions of planets in the sky.

The Milky Way, shown here, is just one of billions of galaxies in the universe.

GLOSSARY

accretion The coming together of material due to gravity to form larger objects.

asteroids Small objects made of rock that orbit around the Sun.

comets Objects made of dust and ice orbiting the Sun that may form a "tail" as the ice melts.

crust The outer layer of a planet.

differentiation The process in which heavy rocks move to the center of a planet and lighter rocks are pushed toward the surface.

eccentric Stretched out from a circular shape; elliptical; not perfectly circular.

equator A circle around Earth that is as far from the North Pole as it is from the South Pole and that divides the planet into two equal halves—the Northern and Southern Hemispheres.

meteors Small objects traveling through space and entering Earth's atmosphere.

nebula A cloud of gas and dust.

observations Acts of carefully watching and listening; the activities of paying close attention to someone or something in order to get information.

oceans Large bodies of salt water on Earth's surface.

orbit To move or travel on a path around an object.

planetesimals Small objects of gas and dust that clumped together to form protoplanets.

rotate To spin around a center point.

solar Of or relating to the Sun.

terrestrial Relating to Earth.

For More Information

Books

Aguilar, David A. *11 Planets: A New View of the Solar System*. Washington, DC: National Geographic, 2008.

Carson, Mary Kay. *Far-Out Guide to the Icy Dwarf Planets*. Berkeley Heights, NJ: Bailey Books/Enslow Elementary, 2011.

Gibbons, Gail. *The Planets*. New York, NY: Holiday House, 2008.

Graham, Ian. *The Near Planets*. Mankato, MN: Smart Apple Media, 2008.

Reilly, Carmel. *The Planets*. New York, NY: Marshall Cavendish Benchmark, 2012.

Sparrow, Giles. *The Outer Planets*. Mankato, MN: Smart Apple Media, 2012.

Websites

Because of the changing nature of Internet links, Rosen Publishing has developed an online list of websites related to the subject of this book. This site is updated regularly. Please use this link to access the list:

http://www.rosenlinks.com/lfo/plan

INDEX